EMMANUEL JOSEPH

The Human Blueprint, Mastering the Art of People Centered Administration

Copyright © 2025 by Emmanuel Joseph

All rights reserved. No part of this publication may be reproduced, stored or transmitted in any form or by any means, electronic, mechanical, photocopying, recording, scanning, or otherwise without written permission from the publisher. It is illegal to copy this book, post it to a website, or distribute it by any other means without permission.

First edition

This book was professionally typeset on Reedsy.
Find out more at reedsy.com

Contents

1	Chapter 1: The Foundation of People-Centered Administration	1
2	Chapter 2: The Role of Empathy in Leadership	3
3	Chapter 3: Building Collaborative Organizational Structures	5
4	Chapter 4: Communication as the Lifeline of Administration	7
5	Chapter 5: Cultivating a Culture of Trust and Respect	9
6	Chapter 6: Emotional Intelligence in Leadership	11
7	Chapter 7: Adaptive Leadership in a Changing World	13
8	Chapter 8: Inclusive Decision-Making	15
9	Chapter 9: Sustainable Organizational Practices	17
10	Chapter 10: The Power of Purpose-Driven Leadership	19
11	Chapter 11: The Future of People-Centered Administration	21
12	Chapter 12: A Roadmap for People-Centered Leadership	23

1

Chapter 1: The Foundation of People-Centered Administration

Administration is often seen as a cold, mechanical process—a system of rules, hierarchies, and procedures designed to keep organizations running. But at its core, administration is about people. It's about understanding the individuals who make up an organization, their needs, aspirations, and challenges. The foundation of people-centered administration lies in recognizing that every decision, policy, and structure impacts real lives. Leaders who embrace this philosophy prioritize empathy, communication, and collaboration, creating environments where people feel valued and empowered.

The shift from traditional, top-down administration to a people-centered approach requires a fundamental change in mindset. It's not just about being "nice" or "soft"; it's about recognizing that human connection drives productivity, innovation, and loyalty. When employees feel seen and heard, they are more likely to contribute their best work. This chapter explores the principles of people-centered administration, emphasizing the importance of trust, transparency, and emotional intelligence in building strong organizational foundations.

One of the key challenges in adopting this approach is overcoming the fear of losing control. Many leaders worry that prioritizing people over processes will lead to chaos. However, the opposite is true. When people feel trusted and respected, they take ownership of their roles and responsibilities, leading to greater accountability and efficiency. This chapter provides practical strategies for balancing structure with flexibility, ensuring that administrative systems support rather than stifle human potential.

The foundation of people-centered administration also involves redefining success. Traditional metrics like profit margins and productivity rates are important, but they don't tell the whole story. True success is measured by the well-being of the people within the organization, their ability to grow, and the quality of their relationships. This chapter encourages leaders to adopt a holistic view of success, one that values both tangible outcomes and intangible human experiences.

By the end of this chapter, readers will understand that people-centered administration is not just a trend or a buzzword—it's a transformative approach that redefines the role of leadership and the purpose of organizational structures. It's about creating systems that serve people, not the other way around.

2

Chapter 2: The Role of Empathy in Leadership

Empathy is often misunderstood as a soft skill, something that's nice to have but not essential for effective leadership. In reality, empathy is a powerful tool that enables leaders to connect with their teams on a deeper level, fostering trust and collaboration. This chapter delves into the role of empathy in people-centered administration, exploring how it can be cultivated and applied in practical ways.

Empathy begins with active listening. It's about setting aside assumptions and truly hearing what others have to say. Leaders who practice active listening create spaces where employees feel safe to express their thoughts and concerns. This not only strengthens relationships but also provides valuable insights that can inform decision-making. This chapter offers techniques for developing active listening skills, such as asking open-ended questions, paraphrasing to confirm understanding, and being fully present in conversations.

Another aspect of empathy is the ability to see situations from multiple perspectives. Leaders who can step into the shoes of their employees, colleagues, and stakeholders are better equipped to make fair and inclusive decisions. This chapter discusses the importance of perspective-taking and provides exercises to help leaders broaden their understanding of different viewpoints.

Empathy also plays a crucial role in conflict resolution. When tensions arise, empathetic leaders focus on understanding the underlying emotions and needs of all parties involved. This approach fosters mutual respect and paves the way for constructive solutions. This chapter includes case studies of leaders who have successfully used empathy to navigate complex conflicts, demonstrating its practical value in real-world scenarios.

Finally, this chapter addresses the misconception that empathy is a fixed trait. While some people may naturally be more empathetic than others, empathy is a skill that can be developed through practice and intention. Leaders are encouraged to reflect on their own empathetic abilities and identify areas for growth. By the end of this chapter, readers will see empathy not as a weakness but as a strength that enhances leadership effectiveness and organizational culture.

3

Chapter 3: Building Collaborative Organizational Structures

Traditional organizational structures often emphasize hierarchy and silos, creating barriers to communication and collaboration. In contrast, people-centered administration prioritizes fluid, interconnected systems that encourage teamwork and innovation. This chapter explores how leaders can design and implement collaborative organizational structures that align with the principles of people-centered administration.

One of the first steps in building a collaborative structure is breaking down silos. Silos occur when departments or teams operate in isolation, leading to inefficiencies and missed opportunities. This chapter provides strategies for fostering cross-functional collaboration, such as creating interdisciplinary teams, organizing regular knowledge-sharing sessions, and using technology to facilitate communication.

Another key element of collaborative structures is decentralization. While traditional hierarchies concentrate decision-making power at the top, decentralized systems distribute authority across the organization. This empowers employees at all levels to take initiative and contribute their unique perspectives. This chapter discusses the benefits of decentralization, including increased agility and employee engagement, and offers guidance on how to implement it effectively.

Collaborative structures also require a culture of trust and accountability. When employees are given more autonomy, they must also be held accountable for their actions. This chapter explores the role of clear expectations, feedback mechanisms, and performance metrics in maintaining accountability while fostering collaboration.

Finally, this chapter emphasizes the importance of adaptability. In a rapidly changing world, organizations must be able to pivot and evolve. Collaborative structures are inherently more flexible than rigid hierarchies, making them better suited to navigate uncertainty. Leaders are encouraged to embrace a growth mindset and continuously refine their organizational structures to meet emerging challenges.

By the end of this chapter, readers will have a clear understanding of how to design and implement collaborative structures that support people-centered administration. They will also recognize the importance of aligning structures with organizational values and goals, ensuring that systems serve the people they are meant to support.

4

Chapter 4: Communication as the Lifeline of Administration

Effective communication is the lifeline of any organization. It's the thread that connects individuals, teams, and departments, enabling them to work together toward common goals. In people-centered administration, communication takes on an even greater significance, as it is the primary means of building trust, fostering collaboration, and ensuring alignment. This chapter explores the role of communication in people-centered administration and provides practical strategies for enhancing communication within organizations.

One of the key principles of effective communication is clarity. Ambiguity and confusion can lead to misunderstandings, mistakes, and frustration. Leaders must strive to communicate clearly and concisely, ensuring that their messages are easily understood by all. This chapter offers tips for improving clarity, such as using simple language, avoiding jargon, and providing context for decisions and instructions.

Another important aspect of communication is transparency. In people-centered administration, transparency builds trust and credibility. Leaders who are open about their intentions, decisions, and challenges create an environment of honesty and integrity. This chapter discusses the benefits of transparency and provides examples of how leaders can practice it in their daily interactions.

Communication is also a two-way street. While leaders must communicate effectively, they must also create opportunities for others to share their thoughts and feedback. This chapter explores the importance of active listening, open forums, and feedback loops in fostering a culture of open communication. It also addresses common barriers to communication, such as power dynamics and cultural differences, and offers strategies for overcoming them.

Finally, this chapter highlights the role of technology in modern communication. While face-to-face interactions are invaluable, technology can enhance communication by bridging geographical and temporal gaps. This chapter provides guidance on choosing and using communication tools effectively, ensuring that technology supports rather than hinders human connection.

By the end of this chapter, readers will understand that communication is not just a functional necessity but a cornerstone of people-centered administration. They will also have practical tools and techniques for improving communication within their organizations, creating a culture of clarity, transparency, and collaboration.

5

Chapter 5: Cultivating a Culture of Trust and Respect

Trust and respect are the bedrock of any successful organization. Without them, collaboration falters, morale declines, and productivity suffers. In people-centered administration, cultivating a culture of trust and respect is not just a goal—it's a necessity. This chapter explores the importance of trust and respect in organizational culture and provides actionable strategies for fostering these values.

Trust begins with consistency. Leaders who consistently act with integrity, follow through on commitments, and treat others fairly earn the trust of their teams. This chapter discusses the role of consistency in building trust and offers tips for maintaining it, even in challenging situations. It also addresses the importance of vulnerability, as leaders who admit their mistakes and seek feedback demonstrate humility and authenticity.

Respect, on the other hand, is about valuing the contributions and perspectives of others. It's about creating an environment where everyone feels appreciated and empowered to speak up. This chapter explores the role of respect in fostering inclusivity and innovation, providing examples of how leaders can demonstrate respect in their words and actions.

Building a culture of trust and respect also requires addressing conflicts and misunderstandings head-on. When trust is broken or respect is lacking, it's essential to address the issue promptly and constructively. This chapter provides guidance on navigating difficult conversations, repairing relationships, and rebuilding trust after a breach.

Finally, this chapter emphasizes the importance of modeling trust and respect at all levels of the organization. Leaders set the tone for organizational culture, but every individual has a role to play in upholding these values. This chapter encourages readers to reflect on their own behaviors and identify ways they can contribute to a culture of trust and respect.

By the end of this chapter, readers will understand that trust and respect are not just abstract ideals but tangible practices that can be cultivated and reinforced. They will also have the tools and insights needed to create an organizational culture where trust and respect thrive, laying the foundation for people-centered administration.

6

Chapter 6: Emotional Intelligence in Leadership

Emotional intelligence (EI) is the ability to recognize, understand, and manage one's own emotions while also being attuned to the emotions of others. In people-centered administration, EI is a critical skill for leaders who aim to create environments where individuals feel understood and supported. This chapter explores the components of emotional intelligence and how they can be applied to enhance leadership effectiveness.

The first component of EI is self-awareness. Leaders who are self-aware understand their strengths, weaknesses, and emotional triggers. This awareness allows them to regulate their emotions and respond to situations thoughtfully rather than react impulsively. This chapter provides exercises for developing self-awareness, such as journaling, mindfulness practices, and seeking feedback from others.

The second component is self-regulation. Leaders with strong self-regulation skills can manage stress, stay composed under pressure, and adapt to changing circumstances. This chapter discusses strategies for improving self-regulation, including deep breathing techniques, time management, and setting boundaries to maintain emotional balance.

Empathy, the third component of EI, has already been explored in Chapter

2, but this chapter delves deeper into its practical applications. Empathetic leaders can build stronger relationships, resolve conflicts, and create inclusive environments. This chapter provides additional tools for cultivating empathy, such as perspective-taking exercises and active listening techniques.

The fourth component is social skills. Leaders with strong social skills excel at communication, collaboration, and conflict resolution. They can inspire and influence others, fostering a sense of unity and purpose within their teams. This chapter offers tips for enhancing social skills, such as practicing assertiveness, building rapport, and celebrating team achievements.

Finally, motivation—the fifth component of EI—refers to the drive to achieve goals and maintain a positive attitude. Leaders who are intrinsically motivated inspire their teams to strive for excellence. This chapter explores the role of purpose and passion in leadership, encouraging readers to align their work with their values and aspirations.

By the end of this chapter, readers will understand that emotional intelligence is not just a personal attribute but a leadership imperative. They will also have practical tools for developing and applying EI in their roles, creating a more empathetic and effective leadership style.

7

Chapter 7: Adaptive Leadership in a Changing World

The world is constantly evolving, and organizations must adapt to survive and thrive. Adaptive leadership is the ability to navigate uncertainty, embrace change, and guide others through transitions. In people-centered administration, adaptive leadership is essential for maintaining resilience and fostering innovation. This chapter explores the principles of adaptive leadership and provides strategies for leading in a dynamic environment.

One of the key principles of adaptive leadership is embracing uncertainty. Leaders who are comfortable with ambiguity can make decisions even when all the answers aren't clear. This chapter discusses the importance of flexibility and experimentation, encouraging leaders to view challenges as opportunities for growth.

Another principle is empowering others to take initiative. Adaptive leaders recognize that they don't have all the answers and rely on the collective intelligence of their teams. This chapter provides strategies for fostering a culture of empowerment, such as delegating authority, encouraging creative problem-solving, and providing resources for skill development.

Adaptive leadership also requires a focus on learning. Leaders must be willing to learn from their experiences, seek feedback, and continuously improve. This chapter explores the role of reflection and feedback in adaptive leadership, offering tools for creating a learning-oriented culture.

Finally, this chapter addresses the emotional aspects of change. Transition can be unsettling, and leaders must be attuned to the emotional needs of their teams. This chapter provides guidance on supporting employees through change, such as communicating openly, acknowledging concerns, and celebrating milestones.

By the end of this chapter, readers will understand that adaptive leadership is not about having all the answers but about navigating uncertainty with confidence and compassion. They will also have practical strategies for leading their organizations through change, ensuring that people remain at the center of the process.

8

Chapter 8: Inclusive Decision-Making

Inclusive decision-making is the practice of involving diverse perspectives in the decision-making process. In people-centered administration, inclusivity is not just a moral imperative but a strategic advantage. This chapter explores the benefits of inclusive decision-making and provides strategies for creating more inclusive processes.

One of the key benefits of inclusivity is better decision quality. When diverse perspectives are considered, decisions are more likely to be well-rounded and effective. This chapter discusses the importance of diversity in decision-making and provides examples of how inclusivity has led to innovative solutions in various organizations.

Another benefit is increased buy-in. When people feel included in the decision-making process, they are more likely to support and implement the decisions. This chapter explores strategies for fostering buy-in, such as soliciting input, explaining the rationale behind decisions, and addressing concerns.

Inclusive decision-making also requires addressing power dynamics. Leaders must ensure that all voices are heard, especially those of marginalized or underrepresented groups. This chapter provides tools for creating equitable decision-making processes, such as rotating facilitators, using anonymous feedback, and setting ground rules for respectful dialogue.

Finally, this chapter emphasizes the importance of transparency and accountability. Inclusive decision-making is not just about involving people in the process but also about being transparent about how decisions are made and holding leaders accountable for their actions. This chapter provides guidance on building trust through transparency and accountability.

By the end of this chapter, readers will understand that inclusive decision-making is not just a checkbox but a transformative practice that enhances decision quality, fosters buy-in, and builds trust. They will also have practical tools for creating more inclusive processes in their organizations.

9

Chapter 9: Sustainable Organizational Practices

Sustainability is often associated with environmental responsibility, but it also applies to organizational practices. In people-centered administration, sustainability means creating systems and processes that support long-term well-being and success. This chapter explores the principles of sustainable organizational practices and provides strategies for implementing them.

One of the key principles of sustainability is balance. Organizations must balance short-term goals with long-term objectives, ensuring that they don't sacrifice future success for immediate gains. This chapter discusses the importance of strategic planning and provides tools for aligning short-term actions with long-term vision.

Another principle is resilience. Sustainable organizations are able to withstand challenges and adapt to change. This chapter explores strategies for building resilience, such as diversifying revenue streams, investing in employee development, and fostering a culture of innovation.

Sustainability also requires a focus on well-being. Organizations that prioritize the physical, emotional, and mental health of their employees are more likely to thrive in the long term. This chapter provides guidance on creating a supportive work environment, such as offering wellness programs, promoting work-life balance, and addressing burnout.

Finally, this chapter emphasizes the importance of ethical practices. Sustainable organizations operate with integrity, ensuring that their actions align with their values and benefit all stakeholders. This chapter provides tools for embedding ethics into organizational culture, such as creating ethical guidelines, conducting regular audits, and fostering open dialogue about ethical dilemmas.

By the end of this chapter, readers will understand that sustainability is not just about survival but about creating organizations that thrive in the long term. They will also have practical strategies for implementing sustainable practices that prioritize well-being, resilience, and ethical responsibility.

10

Chapter 10: The Power of Purpose-Driven Leadership

Purpose-driven leadership is about aligning organizational goals with a higher sense of meaning and impact. In people-centered administration, purpose is a powerful motivator that inspires individuals to contribute their best work. This chapter explores the role of purpose in leadership and provides strategies for cultivating a purpose-driven culture.

One of the key benefits of purpose-driven leadership is increased engagement. When people understand how their work contributes to a larger mission, they are more likely to feel motivated and fulfilled. This chapter discusses the importance of communicating purpose and provides examples of organizations that have successfully aligned their work with a meaningful mission.

Another benefit is resilience. Purpose-driven organizations are better equipped to navigate challenges because they are guided by a clear sense of direction. This chapter explores strategies for maintaining focus on purpose, such as regularly revisiting the mission, celebrating milestones, and sharing stories of impact.

Purpose-driven leadership also requires authenticity. Leaders must embody the organization's purpose and demonstrate a genuine commitment to its values. This chapter provides guidance on leading with authenticity, such as aligning personal and organizational values, being transparent about challenges, and modeling purpose-driven behavior.

Finally, this chapter emphasizes the importance of inclusivity in purpose-driven leadership. A shared sense of purpose can unite diverse individuals and teams, fostering collaboration and innovation. This chapter provides tools for creating an inclusive purpose-driven culture, such as involving employees in defining the mission and ensuring that the purpose resonates with all stakeholders.

By the end of this chapter, readers will understand that purpose-driven leadership is not just about achieving goals but about creating a lasting impact. They will also have practical strategies for cultivating a purpose-driven culture that inspires and unites their teams.

11

Chapter 11: The Future of People-Centered Administration

As the world continues to evolve, so too must the ways in which we lead and administer organizations. The future of people-centered administration lies in embracing emerging trends, technologies, and societal shifts while staying true to the core principles of empathy, collaboration, and human connection. This chapter explores what the future holds for people-centered administration and how leaders can prepare for the challenges and opportunities ahead.

One of the most significant trends shaping the future is the rise of remote and hybrid work. The COVID-19 pandemic accelerated the adoption of remote work, and many organizations are now embracing hybrid models that combine in-person and virtual collaboration. This chapter discusses the implications of remote and hybrid work for people-centered administration, emphasizing the importance of maintaining human connection in a digital world. Leaders are encouraged to leverage technology to foster collaboration while also creating opportunities for meaningful face-to-face interactions.

Another trend is the increasing focus on diversity, equity, and inclusion (DEI). As societies become more diverse, organizations must prioritize DEI to remain relevant and competitive. This chapter explores the role of people-centered administration in advancing DEI, providing strategies for creating inclusive cultures, addressing systemic barriers, and ensuring equitable opportunities for all. Leaders are encouraged to view DEI not as a compliance requirement but as a core value that drives innovation and growth.

The future also brings new challenges, such as the ethical implications of artificial intelligence (AI) and automation. While these technologies offer tremendous potential for efficiency and innovation, they also raise concerns about job displacement, privacy, and bias. This chapter discusses the role of people-centered administration in navigating these challenges, emphasizing the importance of ethical decision-making, transparency, and human oversight. Leaders are encouraged to view technology as a tool to enhance human potential rather than replace it.

Finally, this chapter explores the growing emphasis on sustainability and social responsibility. As climate change and social inequality become increasingly urgent issues, organizations are expected to play a proactive role in addressing these challenges. This chapter provides guidance on integrating sustainability and social responsibility into people-centered administration, such as setting measurable goals, engaging stakeholders, and aligning actions with values.

By the end of this chapter, readers will have a clear understanding of the trends shaping the future of people-centered administration and the steps they can take to prepare for the road ahead. They will also recognize that the future is not something to be feared but an opportunity to create organizations that are more inclusive, innovative, and impactful.

12

Chapter 12: A Roadmap for People-Centered Leadership

The journey toward people-centered administration is not a one-time effort but an ongoing process of learning, growth, and adaptation. This final chapter provides a roadmap for leaders who are committed to mastering the art of people-centered administration. It synthesizes the key principles and strategies discussed throughout the book and offers a step-by-step guide for implementing them in real-world settings.

The first step in the roadmap is self-reflection. Leaders must begin by examining their own values, strengths, and areas for growth. This chapter provides a series of reflective exercises to help readers assess their leadership style, identify their core values, and set personal and professional goals. By understanding themselves better, leaders can lead with greater authenticity and purpose.

The second step is building a strong foundation of trust and respect. This chapter revisits the principles discussed in earlier chapters, emphasizing the importance of empathy, communication, and inclusivity. Leaders are encouraged to create environments where individuals feel valued, heard, and empowered to contribute their best work. Practical strategies for building trust and respect are provided, such as active listening, transparency, and recognizing achievements.

The third step is designing collaborative and adaptive structures. This chapter explores how leaders can create organizational systems that prioritize human connection and flexibility. Readers are guided through the process of breaking down silos, decentralizing decision-making, and fostering a culture of innovation. Case studies and examples are provided to illustrate how these principles can be applied in different contexts.

The fourth step is embedding purpose and sustainability into the organization's DNA. This chapter emphasizes the importance of aligning organizational goals with a higher sense of meaning and impact. Leaders are encouraged to define their organization's purpose, communicate it effectively, and ensure that it resonates with all stakeholders. Strategies for integrating sustainability and social responsibility are also discussed, such as setting measurable goals and engaging employees in the process.

The final step is continuous learning and improvement. People-centered administration is not a destination but a journey. This chapter encourages leaders to embrace a growth mindset, seek feedback, and adapt to changing circumstances. Tools for fostering a culture of learning are provided, such as regular reflection sessions, feedback loops, and professional development opportunities.

By the end of this chapter, readers will have a clear roadmap for implementing people-centered administration in their organizations. They will also recognize that the journey is not always easy but is ultimately rewarding, as it leads to organizations that are more humane, resilient, and impactful.

Conclusion: The Human Blueprint in Action

The Human Blueprint: Mastering the Art of People-Centered Administration is more than a book—it's a call to action. It challenges leaders to rethink traditional approaches to administration and embrace a philosophy that prioritizes human connection, empathy, and collaboration. By doing so, they can create organizations that not only achieve success but also enrich the lives of the people within them.

As you embark on your journey toward people-centered administration, remember that the true measure of leadership is not power or prestige but

CHAPTER 12: A ROADMAP FOR PEOPLE-CENTERED LEADERSHIP

the positive impact you have on others. The human blueprint is not a rigid formula but a flexible framework that can be adapted to fit the unique needs of your organization and the people you serve.

The future of administration is human-centered, and the time to act is now. By mastering the art of people-centered administration, you can build organizations that thrive in an ever-changing world while staying true to the values that make us human.

www.ingramcontent.com/pod-product-compliance
Lightning Source LLC
LaVergne TN
LVHW020743090526
838202LV00057BA/6205